> To Charles and Griselda, hoping that these stories raise a smile or two of recognition, even nostalgia!
> With very best wishes from Michael.
> December 2005. Strasbourg.

Eating for Britain

36 Vignettes of Life in The...

Michael Hall

Illustrations by Pat Knights and Sean Hogan

Gadfly Publications

Eating for Britain
Copyright ©2005 Michael Hall

ISBN 0-9550494-0-7

Drawings Copyright ©2005 Pat Knights ©2004 Sean Hogan

All rights reserved. No part of this publication may be reproduced, stored in a retrieval system, or transmitted in any form or by any means, electronic, mechanical, photocopying, recording or otherwise, without the prior permission of the publisher and copyright owner.
While the principles discussed and the details given in this book are the product of careful consideration, the author and the publishers cannot in any way guarantee the suitability of recommendations made in this book for individual problems or situations, and they shall not be under any legal liability of any kind in respect of or arising out of the form or contents of this book or any error therein.

Published by Gadfly Publications
24B Heath Street
London NW3 6TE

Cover design and illustrations by Pat Knights and Sean Hogan
Design and layout by Farr out Publications <www.farroutpublications.co.uk>

For Sam and Marg

Contents

Foreword	vii
Afrique: Cinq Etoiles	1
The Anglo-Hyphenateds	2
The Annual Review	3
The Austro-Hungarians	4
Bare Bum Diplomacy	5
The Bollinger Man	6
Bore Dodging	7
Dinner for Thirteen	9
A Case of MR	10
A Distressing British National	11
The Casus Belly	12
Eccentrics	13
Eating for Britain	15
The FO's Ju Ju Box	17
A Friend of the Naked Bath	18
The Honoraries	19
Generosity with the Truth	21
From Hero to Zero	23
Knight Starvation	25
Le Châpeau de Mobutu	27
Joke Countries	28
The Kew Bee Pee	29
Party Games	30
Pooling Resources	31
The Rat Pack	32
A Rest for Gavin	33
Spot the Spook	35
Stick to Cricket	37
SOGOP	38
The Square Cyril	39
The Submariners	41
Third World Carlton	43
Writhing for the Float	45
The Toads	47
The Strasbourg Gargoyles	48
Mr Wilkinson	49
Biographical note	51

Foreword

I hope that readers of this selection of sketches and stories taken from life in 'The Diplomatic', as I think it used to be called, will find them entertaining. Some of them take a mildly satirical view of diplomatic life, and its particular, often peculiar, culture, but running through them all, I think, is a good deal of affection, even nostalgia.

The full name of the present day Foreign Office is the Foreign and Commonwealth Office. This mouthful was the result of a merger between the FO and the CO, the Commonwealth Office, in 1968. Within Whitehall the merged department became known as the FCO. It also acquired a nickname: the Fun and Confusion Office. There was certainly a great deal of fun in my time—the Bare Bum Diplomatist really existed, as did the India Office water colourist. As to whether there was a great deal of confusion, the Official Secrets Act, of course, prevents me from saying.

Without the encouragement and enthusiasm of two former members of the Service, this collection would never have been put together: Ann Farr, the editor of *Password*, the FCO Association magazine, and the owner of Farr out Publications, who has edited and designed the book and Pat Knights, *Password's* illustrator, who has done the illustrations. The two magnificent buildings she has drawn so beautifully are the British Residence in Addis Ababa, still very much a going concern I'm pleased to say, and the former British Residence in Kabul, now sadly a ruin. The production has thus been the result of a three cornered collaboration between Wokingham, King's Lynn and Strasbourg. My gratitude to them is immense.

I am also most grateful to Sean Hogan for the delicious portrait of a diplomatic bag taking it easy in a deck chair on a tropic strand, and I am indebted to Chris von Massenbach, formerly of the BCG Düsseldorf, for SOGOP.

I have dedicated this little book to my parents: my late father Edward Hall, known like so many Halls of his generation as 'Sam', and my mother, Margaret Hall, who is now 88. She is known affectionately as 'Marg'. My father was an excellent raconteur and his many letters to me over the years from Mbabane, Nairobi and Henley were models of clarity and precision.

I am particularly indebted to Marg for awakening my interest in stories when I was a young child in South Africa and Swaziland. She read me stories she had written herself and had been broadcast on SABC in Cape Town in the 1940s. My interests in my first nursery school report in 1946 were listed as "lorries, playing monkeys and stories". Very little has changed in the last 60 years.

Lastly, I want to thank my children, Björn and Emily, for their patience and understanding with my frequent and often long absences from England over the years.

And I must give a big bouquet to Birgit Meyer, my companion for the last nine years, who almost from the moment we first met in Frankfurt, encouraged me to keep writing my stories, and still does.

Michael Hall
Strasbourg, October 2005

Afrique: Cinq Etoiles

THE MAJORITY OF PEOPLE IN the Service had little wish to serve in Africa. They associated it with dangers, such as disease, banditry and tribal warfare. But they didn't know what they were missing. Those in the know were a resourceful and resilient breed of men and women who almost would serve nowhere else. Not for them the Chanceries of Europe where the guests arrived early for receptions and sat in their cars looking at their watches until the precise moment came for them to leave their cars, cross the street and press the door bell.

Indeed the main reason many of them liked Africa was that it was the antithesis of Europe. They joined the Service to experience something different and in Africa they certainly got it. If they were lucky enough to be posted to East Africa, they would experience great vistas of plains and woodland full of wild life; or to Southern Africa, spectacular landscapes of mountain and canyon; or to the Congo, one of the last great swathes of rain forest stretching as far as the eye could see.

These Africa hands adjusted quickly to the different rhythm and pace of life which prevail in most African countries. They learned that to stand any chance of getting local dignitaries to their dinner table by 9pm, they had to invite them for 6pm or even 5pm. They also knew that when they arrived for an appointment at a ministry, there was a good chance they would be told that the State Secretary or the Commissioner was "not on seat". And so that report for London would just have to wait another week.

Others coped well with the state of near anarchy prevalent in many places. Before setting off up country they would ring the transport manager at the local brewery to find out how many road blocks had been set up that week on the road going north, and roughly what the going rate was to get through each road block. Sometimes the local rate of inflation was so high that the Kalashnikov-toting road blockers would accept only beer, cigarettes or condoms. The latter they would sell rather than use themselves.

Talking of the local brewery, a friend in the German service told me that once when he was driving from Yaoundé to Douala in his Mercedes, he got into a duel with a very heavily laden brewery lorry which kept trying to pass him in near suicidal situations. Eventually he lured the brewery lorry driver into attempting to pass him on a corner and at a speed that was far too high. Through his rear view mirror, he watched as the brewery lorry careered into the ditch and keeled over. Scores of people appeared as if from nowhere and started looting the beer, several of them leaping up and down and jubilantly giving him the thumbs up to show their gratitude.

Africa was an attractive posting for couples because unlike more advanced places, it offered opportunities for wives to do useful things like nursing, or teaching, or running handicraft classes. In Europe they were often prevented by local labour law or local affluence from finding fulfilling things to do.

And for many bachelors in the days before AIDs the directness of Africa came as a liberation. After a regime of English boarding schools, residential universities and Surrey dinner dances, they found it refreshing to dance the "soukou soukou" to Zairean bands at places like the Starlight Club in Nairobi, or the Cabane Bambou in Lagos, and to meet dancing partners, who instead of announcing as the evening drew to a close, "I promised Mummy I would be back by midnight," would whisper: "Let us go. I am feeling hot."

Above all, the Africa hands came to admire the great cheerfulness of Africa's people in the face of the most terrible adversity, their warmth and their sense of humour.

"All right. I won't charge you the American price. I'll charge you the French price."

"Oh good."

"Good for me. It is more than the American price."

No. There are virtually no continents left which can offer spectacular landscapes, abundant wild life, vibrant music, opportunities to be useful and so many smiles. Some can offer three or even four of these, but none can offer all five. Africa is definitely a case of Five Stars or, as they would say in the bars of Cotonou, "Afrique: Cinq Etoiles".

The Anglo-Hyphenateds

A RETIRED BRITISH AMBASSADOR I met at a reception in the Foreign Office some years ago said to me, "May I give you some advice? In the course of your career, never get involved with the Anglo-Hyphenateds. I should know because I'm the chairman of one. You'd never believe all the intrigue and back biting that goes on!" He was in fact the chairman of the Anglo-Hyphenated for the country from which came the guests of honour for the evening.

The "Anglo-Hyphenateds", friendship societies set up to promote cultural and social links between the UK and other countries, exist in profusion in London: the Anglo-Austrian, the Anglo-French, the Anglo-Turkish and so on.

In addition to the Anglo-Hyphenateds, there are also the Hyphenated-Anglos. These are not, as one might imagine, people with double barrelled names like Hobart-Hampden, Millington-Drake or Barrington-Ward, but the friendship societies abroad. As the name of the host country has to come first in the title, they become the Hyphenated-Anglos: the Franco-Britannique, the Nederland-Engeland, the Egypt-Britain and so on.

Our local Hyphenated-Anglo is the Deutsch-Englische Gesellschaft and it is immaculately run by a board of highly cultured men and women under the chairmanship of a distinguished former member of the German foreign service. No sign of intrigue and back-biting here or, if there is, they keep it well concealed.

We have had some excellent speakers in the time I have been here: Norman Stone, Roger Scruton, and Giles Radice with Quentin Davies doing a double act on the single European currency. Perhaps the most engaging has been John Brookes, the landscape designer, who spoke last night on "The English Garden". Here are some extracts.

"The gentry commissioned these rustic idyll pictures depicting their estate workers all lolling about because they really believed their workers just lolled about—a bit of gentle cow-herding here, some harvesting there. But it wasn't like that at all. The workers toiled from dawn to dusk; they lived in hovels and they fed off messes of potage—a sort of soup. And the only way they could eat red meat was by poaching a hare or a pheasant, and if they were caught they were sent off to Australia."

"Rachel Carson wrote a book in the 1950s called the "Silent Spring" which said these huge single crop acreages were all very well, but they caused the destruction of hedges, and the huge amount of fertiliser they used ended up in our bread and our water and it caused lady birds to have five and a half spots instead of nine."

"Lots of husbands at this time who slaved away every Saturday over the lawn, went for walks in the woods and saw carpets of flowers growing in the glades and said, 'What am I messing about with this lawn thing for? Let the lawn do what it wants!'"

The Anglo-Hyphenateds and the Hyphenated-Anglos might have their detractors, but I am not one of them. I am a firm fan. Without them, I might have continued to have illusions about the lot of estate workers in the 18th and 19th centuries, ruined my Saturdays, my retirement and my back messing about with that lawn thing, and never have learned the correct number of spots on a ladybird.

The Annual Review

Every British ambassador or High Commissioner in the world is required to write an annual review. The whole exercise rather resembles a school essay: it has to be handed in by a certain time and it should not exceed a certain number of words. Generally speaking, but not always, the most diverting ones are written by the heads of post in smaller countries. This is because the further down the country size scale you go, the more life resembles the goings on in a tropical Clochemerle. Here is an example.

The National Day Celebrations. The President's speech was interrupted by a salute of cannons, followed by a deafening fanfare of trumpets which should have taken place before he had started to speak, but the timing of which had slipped. For the march past, the Soviet Ambassador sat down in the most prominent position but, finding the heat oppressive, he moved back into the shade. The American Ambassador then arrived and sat down in the hot seat. The Russian, seeing that he was in danger of being upstaged, moved back to the heat of the front row. I was very glad of our new policy of maintaining a low profile in this area.

Internal. In the absence of any opposition, all news revolves around the doings of the President or the security forces. The President's caution is such that he prepares all food himself—octopus stew is one of his specialities—but he leaves his chief henchman, a shirtless giant called Barbarossa, to stir the pot. In March an exchange of shots between the island's forces and the crew of an unidentified boat near to the mole of the harbour gave rise to an invasion scare. The crew of the suspect vessel were later identified as American marijuana smugglers. In September the Major in charge of the coastguard was dismissed for selling brass from used ammunition. He had been ordering his men to fire on often innocent yachts and deep sea anglers simply for the sake of the empties.

Law and Order. This year saw an outbreak of 'terror shooting'. This consists of firing off a shotgun at windows in residential areas in the middle of the night from a moving bicycle. The culprits are generally aged between 15 and 20. The police and some residents have responded by lying in wait with steel wires stretched across the road. These are pulled taut at the last moment. Following some severe injuries and two decapitations, the incidence of this activity has diminished dramatically.

Relations with Britain. There is considerable good will towards Britain but none of my contacts has a good word to say for the Miss World contest held annually in London. In their view this consistently fails to recognise that the island's metissa is the most beautiful girl on earth. Enormous good will could be generated if a way could be found to include an island girl in at least the last eight. Perhaps the Department could give some thought to this.

The installation of the pool at my Residence has begun to pay considerable dividends. Since it was put in, my contact with the President has increased considerably. He drops in for a swim once or twice a week and we hold discussions while doing lengths. It is now known that the Head of State will not visit diplomats without pools, and the French and the Americans are frantically having pools put in. The Chinese Ambassador will be at some disadvantage, as it is known that he cannot swim.

The Austro-Hungarians

The story is told of Otto von Habsburg who, when he was a member of the European Parliament in the 1980s, was asked during one of his visits to Strasbourg whether he would be watching the Austria-Hungary match, to which his reply was, 'Who are they playing against?'

The Hungarian Ambassador here at the Council of Europe, Count Janos Perenyi, would have been a worthy representative of the Habsburgs at the time when they ruled half of Europe. He is a practitioner of diplomacy in the style of the nineteenth century where unfailing courtesy is combined with the gift of elegant circumlocution.

Not long after I arrived in Strasbourg, I attended a meeting chaired by Ambassador Perenyi. Among the many others present was Ambassador Ulrich Hack, the head of the Austrian delegation. He too would have been a worthy representative of the Habsburgs, his great strengths being infinite patience and unfailing good humour. Towards the end of the discussion on the text, Austria requested the floor.

'Chairman, I do not want to prolong the debate unnecessarily, but I would like to propose two small cosmetic changes to our draft which might bring about some improvement'. Ambassador Hack then read out his amendments.

Count Perenyi replied, 'I am most grateful to the Austrian Ambassador for his most helpful suggestions. One might say that the cosmetics he uses are of the highest quality, Christian Dior or Chanel, if I may say so.'

After Albania, the UK and Ukraine had all looked round to check that the distinguished representative of Austria was not in fact wearing make up, the suggested touches of Hack No 5 were added to the text and it was adopted.

Some days later I was at another meeting chaired by Ambassador Perenyi and there was a 'huits clos' item on the agenda. This is an item for which members of the Secretariat are not allowed to be present and the discussion takes place behind closed doors. As soon as the business on the previous item was completed, the Secretariat got up to leave. After the last of them had gone through the swing doors, Count Perenyi took the floor: 'Ladies and gentlemen, now that the conditions for 'huits clos' have been fulfilled, we can resume our deliberations'.

A mystified colleague, newly arrived from London, asked me for a translation. I replied, 'In plain language it means "Now that the Secretariat's buggered off, we can get down to business", but of course Perenyi can't say that. Always listen to the Austro-Hungarians. You can learn a lot about finesse from them'.

Bare Bum Diplomacy

I HAD A FRIEND IN the Service who had no patience whatever with all the paraphernalia of diplomatic life—ambassadors with large residences, retinues of servants, chauffeur-driven cars, the rounds of receptions, dinners and farewells. All this got in the way of the real work. Also too much of the culture of diplomacy was based on an aristocratic tradition. The worst exponents of this were the British with their practice of conferring titles on ambassadors and senior mandarins. This only exacerbated an existing propensity for heads of post to behave like landed gentry.

And operationally he did not believe in over-large establishments. As soon as you appointed an ambassador, you had to appoint a counsellor: if you had a counsellor, then you had to have two first secretaries and so it went on. And then you had to find premises for all these people to live and work in.

My friend's solution was what he called 'bare foot diplomacy'. Diplomacy shorn of all encrustation—diplomats operating like foreign correspondents, working out of hotel rooms, taking taxis, entertaining selectively in restaurants rather than arranging mass catering for social climbers and spongers. Above all, dips overseas should not be accompanied by spouses. The need to keep bored or homesick spouses happy absorbed far too much of the time and energy of busy officers. For this side of life, diplomats should live off the land. That was what foreign correspondents did.

There have in fact been many occasions in the history of the Service when bare foot diplomacy, along the lines promoted by my colleague, has been practised. These have occurred most frequently when diplomatic relations have suddenly been established with a country but permanent premises not yet found, and so a chargé d'affaires is quickly sent out to present his credentials and to pitch his tent in the best hotel in town: he is without a car and he is unaccompanied. All the essential ingredients of bare foot diplomacy.

But the problem with bare foot diplomacy is that it can all too quickly turn into what another colleague called bare bum diplomacy. Bare foot diplomats are vulnerable; they are, in all senses of the word, exposed. Their telephone calls are liable to be tapped, their papers can be stolen by chambermaids and international hotels swarm with alluring ladies, many of whom are up to no good.

One bare foot diplomat arrived en poste married but was soon in the arms of a 19 year old aspiring journalist he had met in the hotel bar. Another was several times spotted doing some highly selective entertaining in the hotel's grill room by a television team staying in a suite directly above the bare foot diplomat. One warm evening the diplomatist was injudicious enough to entertain his dinner guest in his room with the window open. The television boys lowered a directional microphone and recorded every sound. To the credit of the Service and the admiration of the eavesdroppers, the sounds were both copious and protracted.

No. There are far too many temptations, hazards and pleasures attaching to bare foot diplomacy. BFD may be fine for the licentious press but in the interests of Queen and Country it is far better to lock diplomats into a fortress of official premises, secure communications, rounds of pointless parties and accompanying spouses.

The Bollinger Man

Years ago in Paris there used to be an immaculately dressed and well spoken Englishman who would go up to American women sitting on their own in the bar at the Ritz or the Georges Cinq and introduce himself as the British Ambassador.

'May I join you?' he would say, and the ladies would invariably consent. He would then gaily say, 'Let's have champagne!', order a bottle of Bollinger or Veuve Clicquot and engage the ladies in the most charming conversation.

When the bottle was almost finished, the man would suddenly get up and say, 'Would you excuse me for a moment? I must make a telephone call to the Embassy? I won't be long.' The man may well have telephoned an embassy, and possibly an hotel of that name, but he certainly did not telephone Her Britannic Majesty's Embassy. Nor did he return to the bar, and so the hapless ladies would find themselves landed with a bill for a bottle of Moët et Chandon or Piper-Heidsieck. There then followed irate telephone calls to the British Embassy, but the Private Secretary was always able to account in detail for the real Ambassador's movements.

In the early days of my posting to Frankfurt, before I had built up a social life, I went to the night club attached to the casino in Bad Homburg. Bad Homburg was famous as a fashionable spa resort in the Edwardian era and members of the British and Russian royal families used to go there regularly. I felt that if Bad Homburg had been good enough for them there would be little stigma in my going there.

I danced twice with a tall attractive lady in her late thirties. After the second set, I suggested we had a drink at the bar and ordered a bottle of Henkell Trocken. We embarked on the usual small talk about the casino and the band, and whether one had been there before and so on. Things were developing nicely. We got on to where we worked. She said she worked in the cabinet of one of the directors of Deutsche Bank. I told her that I was the British Consul in Frankfurt.

From that instant on things went rapidly downhill. There was a visible freeze up. Later we parted politely enough but arranging to meet her again I knew was out of the question.

On the drive back to Frankfurt, I puzzled over why she had disengaged so suddenly. Did she consider diplomats very dull? True, we never dropped our guard but within those constraints we could be quite witty. Perhaps she knew that financially we were a dead loss, that we were princes abroad but paupers at home. Or perhaps she had been badly let down by some Consul type in the past. Or there was another possibility: she had heard of the Bollinger man who used to stalk the bars of the Crillon and the Bristol in Paris in the 1960s, posing as the British Ambassador, and she thought I was his nephew.

Bore Dodging

A GREAT DEAL OF EFFORT at diplomatic receptions goes into dodging the bores. All too often you arrive at a national day reception and you run straight into the clutches of a bore. One species of bore hangs around at the entrance to receptions as they know that all guests have to pass through it, rather like cattle passing through a dip, and that therefore it is easy to lay an ambush.

After five minutes of simulated interest and friendliness, you manage to disengage yourself from the entrance bore and you start cautiously to edge your way round the room, hoping to avoid any other bores that might be lying in wait for the unwary. You give the buffet a particularly wide berth because the food tables are the haunt of another species, the buffet bores. The latter know that sooner or later most guests will succumb to hunger or greed and make for the buffet, rather like wildebeest making their way to the waterhole and, as in the animal world, there it is exceptionally easy for a predator to pounce.

Your spirits start to rise, especially as you have spotted two attractive women standing on their own whom you've never seen before, a rarity at national day receptions, and you begin to move in their direction, not too quickly or obtrusively. One is now being predatory oneself. You are almost there when suddenly you hear a voice hailing you. You look round and your worst fears are realised. It is the doyen of the bore corps, and he is bearing down on you. You are transfixed as if darted with a tranquilliser. That tranquilliser is a paralysing substance called diplomatic etiquette, which renders you incapable of ignoring the approaching bore and heading on towards the two gazelles. The super bore says that he wants to discuss the UK position on the sanctions issue. Your heart sinks, not least because he probably knows much more about the UK position on the sanctions issue than you do.

Your heart sinks even further when, out of the corner of your eye, you see the lanky Dutch Chargé reaching the two ladies. You then start to rationalise. You tell yourself that probably the two ladies aren't very interesting anyway, that it would do your reputation no good if you were to be seen talking to unattached ladies and the process of rationalisation goes so far that you decide that you are even grateful to the super bore for having saved you from a step which might have made you the subject of comment. Knowing that earnest conversation is much harder to conduct if the participants have their mouths full, you suggest to the bore baronet that you and he go and have something to eat. You then spend ten minutes in mutually incomprehensible discussion, mouths full of vol au vent, before looking at your watch, pleading a dinner engagement and disappearing into the night. Score: two bores skilfully escaped from and several others successfully avoided.

However as you drive, cycle or walk home, you suddenly have a terrible thought: that perhaps you yourself are an awful bore and that at the reception you have just left there were several people going to great lengths to avoid encountering you, and that you should therefore be very grateful that there had been some people there who had wanted to talk to you.

Dinner for Thirteen

Diplomatic dinner parties are like prototype aircraft: some soar into the air with the greatest of ease, others lumber along the runway for what seems like an eternity and then run into a muddy field. We once gave a dinner that threatened not only never to get airborne, but to collapse even before it got out of the hangar.

After the usual 'va et vient' with acceptances and regrets, we had found ourselves with a party of fourteen: the French, Greek, German and Italian Deputy Heads of Mission and their wives, the Deputy Secretary General and the Russian Chargé and their wives and ourselves. By 8pm most guests had arrived and were drinking aperitifs in the salon. Only the Russians hadn't arrived.

At 8.20 the door bell went. But it wasn't the Russians. It was a Dutch lady who we were sure had declined. An extra place would have to be laid but in no circumstances should she see this happening; so, while I closed the doors between the salon and the dining room, an extra place was hurriedly squeezed on to the end of the table.

Eight-thirty came and went but still no sign of the Russians. We could sense that people were getting restive but if we went through now we would be thirteen. We could go ahead, hoping that no one would notice, but the risk of a sudden shriek half way through the soup followed by people frantically crossing themselves had to be avoided. I said that it was clearly time to eat but unfortunately our Russian colleagues hadn't yet arrived and, if we sat down now, we would be thirteen. If we did so, did anyone mind?

The Frenchman, in a typically Cartesian fashion, said he didn't mind as did the down to earth Dutch lady, and so we went through.

We were just about to take our places when the wife of the Italian Adjoint announced that she was not going to sit down. She had known some people in Rome who had once sat down as thirteen and, two days later, one of them had been found murdered. Encouraged by this, another lady said that she wasn't happy either. She knew a similar story, except it was Bogotá and it was a drowning. I said I quite understood everyone's concerns and that one solution might be for the serving lady to sit with us for the soup course. We would be fourteen and by then the Russians might have arrived. This idea was accepted, but misgivings were discernible on several faces. Clearly those concerned did not think that the evil eye could be so easily deflected by such a feeble subterfuge.

The next problem I had not anticipated. It was also a taboo but one of a quite different order. When I put to the serving lady my fourteenth place proposal, she said she was 'désolée' but she could not possibly sit at the table with the guests. In twenty years of serving she had never sat with the guests. The cook then urgently summoned us to point out that it was now 8.45 and that if we didn't start eating soon, the lamb would be completely dried out.

We were just about to create a second table by taking four places away from the big table and putting them on a table in another room, when the door bell went. The Russians had arrived. Never in my life had I been so happy to see Russians arrive. The rest of the company apparently felt the same way because as the Russians entered the dining room they received the most rapturous applause. The Russians beamed and bowed, clearly assuming that this warm welcome was entirely due to their great personal popularity. The Italian Signora smiled beatifically and crossed herself, the soup was served, glasses were raised and the dinner party was at last cleared for take off.

As for the Dutch lady—to this day she remains blissfully unaware of the palpitations she caused that night.

A Case of MR

The 'locally engaged' are the members of an Embassy's staff who have been recruited locally, as opposed to those who have been recruited in London and sent overseas. It would be very difficult for any Embassy to survive without its 'LE Staff': it is they who have the detailed knowledge of the local culture, the local market for exports and the local bureaucracy. They perform a vital role of illuminating what would otherwise be dark labyrinths, especially for those newly arrived from London.

There used to be an aristocracy amongst the locally engaged but they are no more. These were the Oriental Secretaries. The OSs, often British, were people who had grown up in the country, and were recruited for their immense knowledge of local politics and history. They served in the political sections and provided an invaluable element of continuity, but they were phased out some years ago, possibly because some Ambassadors found them alarmingly knowledgeable and therefore a threat.

I know of one Ambassador, however, who much regretted their passing. He said that he would not have got his prediction on the survival chances of the Shah of Iran wrong if he had had an Oriental Secretary. The OS would have reminded him of the great historical power of the mullahs, and how they had stopped a gargantuan scheme to plant tobacco in Persia in the 1920s.

The vast majority of locally engaged staff are loyal, hard working and conscientious, and many feature in the Honours Lists each year. Some members of the Diplomatic Service even owe their lives to the bravery of locally engaged staff but, as in any large cadre of people, there will inevitably be a handful who are up to various little rackets and swindles. Or, put more euphemistically, there are from time to time cases of misdirected resourcefulness, otherwise known as 'MR'.

The best known case of MR in recent times was the accountant in a Middle East country who kept twenty local British pensioners alive well into their nineties. For years London accepted the extraordinary longevity of these people, attributing it to the desert air and a diet of figs and honey but, when four of the pensioners turned a hundred, London's curiosity was aroused. An investigation revealed that 15 of the 20 had in fact died, in some cases several years previously, and that the accountant had kept them alive so that he could build himself a villa with a swimming pool and live in some style. A long period then ensued in his life when he saw neither house nor pool, nor much sky for that matter.

It was reckoned that if he had settled on a slightly smaller villa and had allowed the twenty to die off gradually in their eighties, he might well have been lolling on his lilo, instead of sewing policemen's berets. One consequence of his life prolonging activities is that British pensioners living abroad now have at regular intervals to go to their nearest British Consulate and swear that they are still alive—an act of near perjury in many cases.

A Distressing British National

Last week a British subject arrived at the reception of the Frankfurt Consulate, which is located on the 8th floor of Triton Haus in the Bockenheimer Landstrasse, and said that he had just thrown up in the lift. He had also lost his money and his passport.

While our consular clerk attended to the unfortunate man, a meeting was hastily held in the Vice-Consul's office to discuss what should be done about what the DBN (Distressed British National) had done in the lift. Our hard liner said the man should be given a bucket and mop and asked to clean it up himself. The majority considered this was out of the question; the man was clearly ill and he had lost his money. We were a sanctuary, not a penal colony or a British boarding school.

Our hard man then suggested that Deutsche Bank should be asked to clear it up: the mess had landed on Deutsche Bank territory (Triton Haus is a Deutsche Bank building) and cleaning the common parts of the building was a landlord's responsibility. The same majority thought it most unlikely that Deutsche Bank would agree to this. The bank would be bound to argue that the cleaning was our responsibility as it was the deed of a British subject on his way to see us which had put the lift out of action and that when they had accepted the Consulate as a tenant, they had not anticipated that we would have visitors who threw up in the lifts.

Towards the end of the meeting the telephone rang. It was the Hausmeister of Triton Haus: one of the lifts had been rendered unfit for human occupation and the probability, without disrespect to the British Consulate, was that one of the Consulate's more unfortunate visitors was responsible. The Vice-Consul confirmed that one of our consular cases had indeed been ill in the lift and the Consulate would accept responsibility for cleaning it up.

Our hard liner said we had capitulated too easily. We should have said the lift could just as easily have been contaminated by one of the American lawyers, Japanese bankers or German estate agents also working in the building. Of course, this was unlikely, but at least the administration of the building should not be allowed to assume that every unfortunate or unpleasant thing which happened in the building could be attributed to the British. Our Vice-Consul said the sad fact had to be faced that invariably this was the cause.

The Casus Belly

IN DIPLOMACY THINGS ARE FREQUENTLY not what they seem. Indeed, most of the time they are not what they seem. When the Malvolian Ambassador says that he is delighted to see you, you can be pretty sure that he is not in the least bit delighted to see you, and equally when you say you are delighted to see him, the chances are that you are just as unenthusiastic.

But there are sound practical reasons for all this dissembling, the principal one being to avoid war. If you were to say to the Malvolian, 'Good morning, you loquacious old bore!' it could become a 'casus belli'. Peace based on insincerity is infinitely preferable to war based on plain speaking.

Dissembling can, however, occur for reasons very different from the need to avoid war—to save face, for instance. There was an episode in one of my postings where face was at stake, although the central issue was in fact a belly, rather than a face—a 'casus belly' one might say. The belly belonged to the Chairman of a leading British international institution and its owner was due to come and give a talk to an invited audience of local worthies. We proposed that the host for the occasion would be our Ambassador, the venue his Residence and that the talk would be followed by a buffet supper.

We thought that there could not possibly be any objections to such an attractive scenario, but we were wrong. The Chairman's office in London said that the Chairman deserved a bigger audience than could be fitted into the Residence. Could the event not be held at a club or an hotel with a proper sit down dinner?

We were astonished. We pointed out that this would change the whole character of the occasion. Clubs and hotels were distinctly impersonal places and the response was likely to be far better if the venue were the Residence. Moreover people would think it decidedly odd if the Ambassador were to be the host at an event in an hotel. They might wonder whether he had been evicted or had something to hide, like a ghastly collection of paintings or a transsexual housekeeper.

But the Chairman's office was adamant. The Chairman was a very important person, the net for invitations should be cast very wide and a large audience assembled. We were amazed at this degree of self-importance. We decided that we should not allow ourselves to be pushed around. The Chairman could take our offer or leave it.

Clearly seeing the prospect of a visit to an attractive European city disappearing fast, the Chairman's office rapidly backed down. 'The Chairman is very happy to accept the Ambassador's proposals for the evening and he looks forward to it very much. To be absolutely candid, the problem has been the buffet supper. The Chairman is rather stout, I'm afraid, and so has great difficulty in balancing plates on his knees. Could he possibly be provided with a small table for the meal?'

We were tempted to point out that the problem had clearly not been our Ambassador's buffet but their chairman's belly, but we decided against such provocation. We said of course we could provide a small table and with that the day was saved. The chairman came, spoke to great acclaim and ate and drank at his own little table. No one considered this the slightest bit odd and the following morning he and his belly flew contentedly back to England.

Eccentrics

The word 'eccentric' means 'away from the centre' or 'outside the norm'. The Foreign Service in its time has produced a fair crop of eccentrics but as private incomes have become a thing of the past, and as London's control over posts and staff has grown ever tighter, eccentrics have become a vanishing breed.

It is noticeable that often the further away people are from the centre, the more eccentric they become. There was the Consul in the Cameroons who found the heat so intolerable in the hot season that he used to work sitting in a bath of cold water. The files would be brought up to his house by the clerks and placed on a wooden board stretched across the bathtub. In the early evening, he would go down to his office to return telephone calls. Churchill also used to work from his morning bath, but he would dictate to stenographers from behind a screen. A screen would have been no good to our man for preserving his modesty so he wore a bathing costume.

And there was the Chargé in Peking who was a passionate grouse moors man. There were plenty of pheasant in the hills around Peking but because the Chinese forbade the importation of gun dogs, the Chargé would ask the Third and Second Secretaries to act as his beaters and retrievers. Of course, as the Chargé countersigned all their annual reports, they didn't have much choice. The Chargé's aim was none too good so each time these young men heard a salvo behind them, they would immediately throw themselves to the ground, much to the irritation of the Chargé.

But the centre could also produce eccentrics. There was the Legal Adviser in London who towards the end of his career took up watercolours and spent most of his day painting in his office which had a view of St James's Park. Anyone going round to see him to discuss a problem would be greeted with, 'Never mind about that. Come over here. Do you think that I need to darken the sky a bit ?'

This man was greatly liked by junior staff as he had a reputation for siding with the underdog, whether it was a state, a tribe or an individual. On one occasion, the Administration had wanted to sack a clerk and a secretary who had been caught by a security guard having congress on the table in the room in which the Treaty of Locarno had been signed. But the Administration was also anxious to avoid a complaint of unfair dismissal and had consulted the Legal Advisers. The water colourist's response on the lengthy minute he'd received was, 'I don't think these young people should receive anything harsher than a lesson in table manners.'

If this delightful man were still in the FO, in this age of personal objectives, self appraisals and performance related pay, I have no doubt that his top personal objective would be 'painting twelve studies of St James's Park in different light conditions for each month of the year'.

Eating for Britain

EVEN ONLY A MODERATELY SUCCESSFUL diplomat, by the time he reaches retirement, will have eaten his way through several hundred official dinners and lunches during the course of his career. For those who reach the top of the Service, the number of meals they will have survived will run into several thousand. Our Ambassadors in Paris, Washington and Berlin spend at least a quarter of their waking hours eating for Britain.

On the face of it being sent abroad to eat for your country would seem to be many people's idea of bliss, but one really can have too much of a good thing. My Ambassador in one post would look at his programme in the morning and, on seeing that he was lunching with the Transylvanians and dining with the Lilliputians, would cry out, 'Oh God! Not more unwanted calories! If the Foreign Office expects us to eat all these meals, it really ought to be prepared to send us to a health farm once a year and pay for our suits to be let out!'

Often these deadly gastronomic rounds are driven by the demands of reciprocity. When you arrive in post, you receive many invitations from the Corps. First, they want to welcome you as a new 'cher collègue' and second, they want to check you out. Do you play bridge? Do you play tennis? What were your previous postings? Then, of course, in time you have to reciprocate—and the game of social ping pong begins and escalates.

A great deal of eating (and drinking) for one's nation takes place at receptions and at national day parties. In a large diplomatic community there can on average be one of these a week. It is of course essentially the same party: even the waiters and the canapés can be the same. The only things that change are the venue and the flag flying on the pole outside. But national day parties are one of the inescapable rituals of the diplomatic merry go round.

One does, regrettably, come across the occasional member of the Corps who does not eat for his country but for himself. This is very bad form. There was one notorious case of EFO (Eating for Oneself) in one of my postings. The man was an Ambassador and single and seemingly his country could not afford to provide him with a cook because he would seize every gastronomic opportunity to tank up and stock up.

He was moreover by far the shortest member of the Corps which enabled him to dart into the mêlée around the buffet table, and shovel the food directly into his mouth under the noses of his taller colleagues. His First Secretary, the most urbane of men, would squirm with embarrassment. He'd spot his diminutive boss hoovering up the quails eggs or the devils on horseback, and pray that he'd be taken for some famished gate crasher. But unfortunately the Chef de Mission and his exploits were far too well known.

The hapless First Secretary would then go to the other extreme, and eat virtually nothing at receptions and dinners in order to make it quite clear that not all the representatives of his country were gluttons and freeloaders. Hardly corpulent when arrived in post, he was virtually emaciated by the time his posting was up. Now if he'd been British, he would have been a case of starving for Britain.

The FO's Ju Ju Box

EVERY HUMAN ORGANISATION HAS AN object which it imbues with almost mystical significance. With a regiment it is the colours, with a grand family its coat of arms, with an African tribe it may be the skull of Mamba, the giant crocodile. In the Foreign Office's case it is the Diplomatic Bag.

Essentially this is a canvas bag, not unlike a sailor's kit bag, with a series of small brass portholes around the neck to enable it to be secured with strong twine and then sealed. Across the body of the bag are emblazoned the words 'Property of Her Britannic Majesty's Diplomatic Service'. The implicit warning in these words is clear.

This mundane object's mystical significance derives from the fact that it is the means by which all manner of secret letters, memos and packages are conveyed from London to posts all over the world, and from those same posts back to London. It is the link between the mother ship and her vessels scattered across the globe. And there are elaborate rules on what may and may not be put in the bag, another testimony to its semi-sacred status. The tribe worshipping Mamba the giant crocodile would definitely describe the bag as the FO's Ju Ju Box.

The bag's mystique is enhanced by the fact that it is carried by a team of Queen's Messengers, many of them former officers in the Queen's armed services. Indeed, so important is the bag, it gets a first class seat of its own on aeroplanes, and the power of the bag is such that the lives of the posts overseas revolve around its arrival and departure. Its imminent arrival is looked upon with distinctly mixed feelings. It may bring letters from loved ones; it may also bring instructions from the Department requiring an enormous amount of action. Conversely it can bring bad news from home and good from the Office. The whole gamut of human life can be lurking in the depths of the bag.

And an Embassy's graph of activity follows precisely the movements back and forth of its bag service. Activity is at its lowest level just after the departure of a bag, but it starts to rise as the next Bag Day approaches. It reaches fever pitch on the eve of Bag Day and, in the case of some officers, a crescendo on the day itself. This is the day the secretaries dread most, when the Embassy's procrastinators finally bestir themselves. Indeed some officers, it seems, are only able to perform with the guillotine of the bag's closure time hovering over them. Perhaps they conduct their conjugal lives on the same principle.

The diplomatic bag and its contents are not something to be trifled with. The scene is the OBR (Outward Bag Room) which is one of the two engine rooms in the Foreign Office, (the other being the Telegraph Room). Here bags are filled, logged, sealed, weighed and despatched.

One day the OBR received a note from an Ambassador's wife who was doing good works in a third world country. She wrote that she had ordered twelve gross of condoms for a project on family planning she was running, but only one gross had arrived. She had contacted the firm supplying them and they would be sending the missing eleven to the OBR for despatch.

The eleven gross duly arrived but, before sealing them in the bag, one of the clerks put in a note which read, 'Dear Lady B, Please find enclosed the balance of the French letters you ordered. I'm sure that the weekend will now be a great success. My best wishes to Sir Roger.'

Unfortunately Lady B had a taste only for good works and none for humour, for she demanded that HE write a complaint to the Head of the Outward Bag Room. The clerk found himself despatched out of the OBR and almost out of the Foreign Office, which shows that the diplomatic bag and its contents, if not treated with the utmost respect, can be as dangerous as the skull of Mamba, the giant crocodile.

A Friend of the Naked Bath

SOME GOVERNMENTS SPEND HUGE SUMS of money on devices to decode the coded communications of their competitors and their potential enemies. Regrettably, it is even sometimes necessary for them to try to read the correspondence of their friends—if they think that their friends may be up to no good.

But not only governments need to have diplomatic decoding devices. Diplomats also need to possess them. Not some elaborate electronic device devised in Cheltenham or Bletchley but a facility which the diplomat carries in his head at all times, both when he is on and off duty.

The block of flats where I lived when I was posted to Frankfurt was equipped with a Schwimmbadanlage, that is, an area containing a swimming pool, a small gym and a sauna. One evening, not long after I had arrived in post, I was swimming up and down the small pool doing backstroke when two ladies in their thirties entered the pool area, looked briefly in my direction and disappeared into the sauna, I assumed in order to have a sauna, but they emerged a few minutes later stark naked. Without looking in my direction they lowered themselves into the pool. I have to admit that I was looking in theirs.

Now some might think that this was an enviable situation for a man to find himself in, alone in a pool with two well-proportioned, naked ladies. On the contrary, the atmosphere was distinctly uncomfortable. The two sexes swam up and down, studiously avoiding each other. The silence was eventually broken by one of the ladies who, as she drew level with me, said in German, 'We assume you do not object that we are both naked?'

My inbuilt diplomatic decoding device immediately deciphered this to mean that the lady and her friend were not happy with a situation which could only be described as oriental—one clad male and two unclad females in a tiled pool with pots of tropical plants. Furthermore, they had no swimwear which they could put on, whereas I had some I could take off. The implication was clear, I had to remove mine. This I did with a quick manœuvre underwater, followed by a lob of my trunks onto the side of the pool.

There was an immediate change for the better in the atmosphere—a critical inequality had been removed. The discarding of the costume did, however, force on me a change of swimming stroke, from back to side stroke.

I inferred from this episode that the etiquette of the Schwimmbadanlage was swimming without costumes. The decisive factor in Germany I deduced is whether the pool has a sauna en suite or not, which proved correct because a day or two later I encountered Herr Kerchnawe, the Hausmeister, at the pool. On seeing me with no costume, he said with evident approval, 'Ah Herr Hall! I see that you are now a friend of the naked bath!'

Now without my diplomatic decoding device, honed at a hundred receptions and dinners, I would never have been admitted to the Friends of the Naked Bath.

The Honoraries

One of the chores of consular life is attending national day receptions. The core guest list for these functions is always the same: all the members of the corps, councillors from city hall, officials from the chamber of commerce and people whom we all need to say thank you to, such as policemen, doctors and the ladies from the VIP lounge at the airport. Essentially it is the same party repeated many times a year, it is only the venue that changes.

In my experience, the Honoraries give by far the best of these parties. The honorary consuls are mostly wealthy local businessmen and lawyers and so can afford to push the boat out. Also, not being career diplomats, they are less inhibited about doing anything unconventional. And the best of the Honorary bashes here in Frankfurt are given by the jolly Herr Muck, the honorary Consul of the Maldive Islands, and by the suave and enigmatic Herr Bruno Schubert, the honorary Consul-General of Chile.

Herr Muck gives his party in the garden of his rambling house on the outskirts of Bad Homberg. The house has a turret, Schloss Muck you might say, and the garden, like Herr Muck himself, is pleasantly dishevelled. The party is always held in August when the weather is positively Maldivian, and it has all the features of a good beach party: barbecues grilling prawns and kebabs, an open air bar and a band serenading the guests. There is also entertainment: fire-eaters, conjurers and two belly dancers—one Turkish and one German. The great regret of those taking their summer leave in August is that they will miss Herr Muck's Maldives party.

It is, incidentally, extremely rare to encounter any actual Maldivians at their national day reception because there are virtually none living in Germany. Herr Muck's consular role is confined to sorting out the problems which ensue when ladies from Hamburg or Hannover decide to bring back to Europe the nice fisherman they met on their diving holiday on one of the atolls, and both parties then run out of things to say to each other.

The Chilean party offers exotic touches of a different sort—Singhalese waiters in white uniforms and gloves glide among the guests, offering drinks and snacks, while emus, wallabies and tropical birds move about the garden, unperturbed by the large invasion of humans. The presence of the emus is not indicative of any particular passion for the European Monetary Union on the part of Herr Schubert, but for wild life conservation. He stands under a tree impassively greeting his guests, exchanging a few words with each new arrival and ushering them on to mingle with the consuls and the emus.

Generosity with the Truth

THERE WAS A TIME WHEN the Foreign Service was run rather like the Army, and officers were simply informed about where their next posting would be. Nowadays things could not be more different—all postings are filled on a purely volunteer basis.

To ensure that you have volunteers for the world's hell holes, you cannot afford to be too generous with the truth about them, which means that today's Foreign Office Post Reports are mean little documents on one side of paper. In the old days, they were veritable pieces of travel literature in which no punches were pulled. If the poor swine heading for Kinshasa or Mogadishu have no choice, then you can afford to tell it exactly how it is. Here is a typical FO Post Report from the 1970s.

Climate. The climate for ten months of the year is oppressively hot but, during the months of July and August, not only is the weather relatively cool, but the absence of a large part of the French population on leave in Europe makes it possible to park one's car and find a seat in the restaurants.

Dress. Because of the stickiness of the climate, it is a good idea to have dresses which are not tight fitting and are easy to get out of (e.g., zipped down the back). This can be practical in a variety of circumstances. Feet swell in the hot weather, so shoes half a size bigger than normal should be brought out.

Nannies. Local nannies do not provide stimulating company for older children and representational officers are entitled to bring out a nanny, but they should check with Personnel Services Department how long their entitlement to a UK nanny lasts. There is no social life for young, single, European girls—at least, not of a conventional kind.

Cars. As of January, the Government has insisted upon all town taxis being painted the shade of yellow commonly known in Europe as mustard. It is not therefore advisable to bring a car of this colour into the country.

Recreation. There is bathing but it is best confined to the faster moving stretches of the river as crocodiles live in the reeds and dislike sharing them with humans. There are two or three night clubs which, while poor by usual standards, are nevertheless frequented by foreigners. They have no floorshow but usually have a band and a space for dancing. Mildly indecent books are very hard to obtain, and officers should bring in enough stocks to last a 12 month tour. For all imported goods worth more than £5, a diplomatic franchise is necessary. This consists of passing a thousand franc note to the warehouseman. There is also a flying and parachute club at the airport where people practise for rapid exodus from the country.

Medical. The Embassy holds stocks of anti-malaria prophylactics and some antidotes to diarrhœa, but those coming here should be warned that Yugundu tummy generally does not respond to drugs. Those unused to French medical practices should be prepared for the frequent and massive doses of antibiotics invariably administered by suppository. Some people tend to get run down towards the end of a 12 month tour and find that it helps to take vitamin pills. There is a burial ground at Bel-Air which is open to all denominations.

THE WORLD HE LEFT BEHIND

From Hero to Zero

Sooner or later, the fateful day dawns when the FO man has to leave the Service and retire. One moment he is the occupant of a large house with wide verandahs and several servants, the possessor of a fulfilling job with a grand title and access to politicians, newspaper editors and tycoons. The next he is in a cottage in Wiltshire, steeling himself to mow his own lawn, wondering if he can afford a case of chablis and barely with access to the local golf club. This transition from prominence to obscurity is known as going from hero to zero.

Some manage the transition with great aplomb and continue in the heroic mould. Leaping effortlessly across the chasm that separates the public service from the real world, they move from running embassies to running charities, to sitting on the boards of large companies or into the headships of Oxbridge colleges. Many are greatly assisted in making this leap by a pair of magical wings known as a knighthood.

Others, sadly, crash miserably to earth and pace up and down like tigers, caged after years of roaming the plains. They compose letters to *The Times*, write memoirs whose publication they are likely to have to finance themselves, and they bully people in the local parish council. Their unfortunate wives have much to contend with.

Others take to the freedom with enormous relish, eschewing the pursuit of directorships, the writing of letters to newspapers and the bullying of their intellectual and social inferiors. Instead they fish or travel, hike or paint, or resume going to the cinema, or cycle round looking for discarded bottles to put in their local bottle bank.

There are yet others who say to hell with everything and decide to do virtually nothing. One such was an Under-Secretary who for the first month of his retirement employed the village paper boy to knock on his bedroom door every morning and cry, 'Watts! Watts! The Minister wants you!' To which Watts would say, 'Tell the Minister to bog off!' and then turn over and go back to sleep again.

But there have been cases of people who have neither continued to fly high nor crashed into the depths, but instead have ascended on retirement from obscurity to celebrity. The most spectacular example was a man who only reached the middle ranks of the Service but who after retirement became a best selling author, able to afford large houses in Norfolk and Tuscany.

He wrote under a *nom de plume* because, he said, he feared that he wouldn't hit the big time if he wrote under his own name. He said that, as they browsed round Hatchards in the lunch hour, the FO's grandees would say, 'He wasn't any good at drafting when he was in the Office. I'm sure he hasn't got any better!' But thanks to the assumption of a new identity that placed him beyond the reach of the grandees, and to a refusal to let the bland prose of Whitehall destroy his personal writing style, he became a case of going from Zero to Hero.

Knight Starvation

THERE WAS A TIME WHEN it was fashionable for British doctors to attribute all kinds of ailments to what was called 'night starvation'. The theory was that the hours of sleep were far too long a period for the human organism to endure without sustenance. Nourishment was therefore needed for the nocturnal journey through this nutritional desert. These doctors would prescribe hot, nourishing, bedtime beverages called Ovaltine and Horlicks to their patients, to be drunk each night before retiring.

The Diplomatic Service has its own variant of knight starvation, except that what the sufferer hungers for is not a cup of Horlicks or Ovaltine but a knighthood before retiring, and a knighthood is hungered for because it is a passport to a world of company directorships, golf club chairmanships and the boards of charities offering plenty of overseas travel.

The ailment is most prevalent in those middle ranking countries where the bestowing of a knighthood on Her Majesty's Ambassador can happen, but where it is far from being a certainty. No traces of the condition are to be found in Paris, Washington, Rome or Berlin, where a K is a dead cert for HMA. And it certainly does not occur in Mogadishu or Managua where the only K anyone has heard of is a Kalashnikov. But the ailment lurks and seethes in the Oslos, Santiagos and the Bangkoks of the British diplomatic world, those marginal posts in the 'K' stakes.

The commonest symptom is hyperactivity on the part of the sufferer. Streams of telegrams are despatched, rounds of dinner parties held (especially for influential visitors from England) and barrages of reports sent from all sections of the Embassy. The entire Embassy staff is harnessed to secure the one elixir which will put the sufferer out of his misery.

Of course, in some cases, the really perceptive doctor will detect that it is not His Excellency who has the bad case of knight starvation, but his wife, and that the gratification she yearns for is not nocturnal but diurnal. A gratification that can be enjoyed whenever tables are booked at The Savoy, goods are paid for at Harrods or applications made to join Hurlingham. It is often she, not some inner demon, who is driving HE down the yellow brick road to Buckingham Palace.

Serving in a post infected with knight starvation can be as bad as serving under Bligh on the Bounty. Each time the New Year or Birthday honours list is published, the First Secretaries, like so many shipwrecked mariners desperately looking out for a passing ship, will scan *The Times* and *The Guardian*, hoping against hope to find their man's name amongst the KCMGs, KCVOs or KBEs.

If their man's name is there, a great whoop of joy goes up, 'The old man's Horlicks has arrived!' they cry. Champagne is opened, ties are loosened and feet are put on desks for the first time in months. They know that the lash will be withdrawn and something resembling a civilised rhythm of life will return to the Chancery.

Le Châpeau de Mobutu

There was a time when wearing a club, school or regimental tie to which one was not entitled was considered a grave social offence, but this taboo is totally disregarded these days.

Indeed the situation has reached the point where when you see someone wearing your old school tie, there's more than half a chance that he has wandered into a shop in Jermyn Street and picked out several school ties, yours among them, and the shop has sold them to him, no questions asked. The fellow might be a Wykhamist on a Monday, a Harrovian on a Tuesday and a Carthusian on a Wednesday. And the fellow in question might not even be British. I once saw an Old Rugbian tie around a neck in Frankfurt.

Things have got even more out of hand. Continental and Far Eastern tie manufacturers are now simply copying the designs of certain British club and college ties and selling them by the thousand to those aspiring to 'le style anglais'. Yesterday morning, for instance, Zobert, our driver at the UK Delegation in Strasbourg, appeared at the office wearing the tie of my school, the King's School, Canterbury. (Canterbury was not, I am afraid, one of those schools where the parting words of house masters to school leavers was, "We don't really mind what you do in life, as long as you excel at it. But we do have one request—please don't wear the tie in Court." This apparently used to be said to all Etonians on their last day at the school in the 1930s, but it may of course be a gross calumny). Back to Zobert. I thought that one of my predecessors might have given him the tie but on closer inspection it proved to be a replica, broader and a touch flashier than the genuine article.

'Ah Zobert,' I said, 'do you know that today you are wearing the tie of my old school in Canterbury in England?'

'Vraiment?' replied Zobert. 'C'est une cravate très classique! Alors, je suis un English gentleman!'

'Certainly,' I said, 'and if you were wearing the tie of Eton College, the most prestigious college in England, you would be un English Lord.'

'Comment est cette cravate de cet Eton College? Est-ce que c'est comme la peau d'un léopard? Comme le châpeau de Mobutu?'

'Non. Ce n'est pas comme le châpeau de Mobutu,' I said, 'ce n'est pas si exotique que ça. Mais c'est une très bonne idée. Je vais la proposer au Directeur de Eton College.'

And it was very good idea. In all probability the Lancaster House Conference on Zimbabwe would not have dragged on nearly as long as it did in 1979 if Lord Carrington had been wearing a leopard skin tie instead of the sober dark and light blue stripes of the Old Etonian tie or, better still, if he had been wearing un Châpeau de Mobutu.

Joke Countries

YEARS AGO I WORKED IN the Department in London which looked after the Foreign Office's official visitors, people from all over the world invited by our posts to spend a week or ten days in Britain at HMG's expense. They would attend Question Time in Parliament, have lunch with MPs, have a call at the FO, visit some firms and then fly up to Scotland. Then back to London for a show like 'Hair' or 'Cats' and perhaps a reception, and away. The idea was to introduce them to Britain in the hope they would leave more pro-British than when they arrived—or at least less anti-British.

Our Head of Department divided the places from which these visitors came into 'proper countries' and 'joke countries'. The latter had this sobriquet for a reason which would nowadays be considered quite unacceptable, which was that they were tiny and newly independent and therefore could not be taken entirely seriously. But there was another reason. The people from these countries did not take themselves very seriously and so they were invariably much more fun to be with.

During a visit by three members of the King's Council from one of these countries, their High Commissioner telephoned the FO to say that the three had to report that afternoon to stand by for a telephone call from their King. Our Head of Department said he was very reluctant to cancel the afternoon's programme. The firm (manufacturers of tractors) always laid on a very good tea. The High Commissioner would have to find three people to stand in. The High Commissioner had instantly agreed and sent round his father in law and two members of his staff. All three played their parts very well, everyone had a ride on a tractor, the tea included doorstep sandwiches and everyone was happy.

Another visiting group consisted of four chiefs from a small, landlocked mountainous country and two things fascinated them—the sea and any form of underground transport, both being totally absent from their country. When this became apparent at the meeting to discuss the tour programme, our Head of Department said, 'What's the point of making these chaps traipse round Whitehall when what they really want to do is see the sea and travel on the Circle Line?'

And so part of the programme had been cancelled and tickets bought for a day trip to Calais as well as passes for the Underground. Although, subsequently, one of the chiefs was ill on the way back from Calais and another had got separated from the main party at Oxford Circus, the FO escort reported that the tour was going splendidly. On their last day the chiefs visited the Commonwealth Institute, travelled through the Blackwall Tunnel and attended a reception at Carlton Gardens.

On departure the chiefs were profuse with their thanks to the Foreign Office, with invitations to go pony trekking in their mountains. As they climbed into the limousine for the journey to Heathrow airport, our Head of Department remarked, 'Very sad that all that spontaneity will go when they turn into a proper country'.

The Kew Bee Pee

While other embassies have a National Day reception which always falls on the same date, the British have the Queen's Birthday Party, or QBP. The QBP has no fixed date—embassies have discretion to choose a date in the second week in June—and the Queen's Birthday isn't in June at all, it's in April. The purpose behind all this pragmatism is to give the event the best chance of success. The ideal QBP is held in a large garden, accompanied by a military band and plenty of sunshine.

But QBPs have become increasingly elaborate and the preparations for them absorb a great deal of a Post's time. Last year's guest list is carefully examined to see who accepted and turned up, who accepted but didn't turn up, and who neither replied nor turned up. Lists are circulated round the embassy for proposals for additions and deletions. A great deal of thought goes into striking a balance between leading locals and members of the British expatriate community. Eventually a definitive list is agreed and the secretaries commence the great chore of filling in the crested cards and addressing envelopes.

Having sent out its invitations, the Post's staff then put on their tin helmets, ready for the telephone calls from members of the British community complaining that so and so has received an invitation to the QBP and they haven't, and that far too many foreigners are being invited these days—the event was designed for Her Majesty's loyal subjects, not for foreigners. Never mind that often the foreigners are working for British companies while many of HM's loyal subjects have never paid UK income tax in their lives.

One is tempted to give these moaners the answer which a Governor-General in India gave when an agitated ADC told him that a particular lady was very unhappy with where she had been placed for a dinner that evening, 'If she matters', said the G-G, 'she won't mind, and if she minds, she doesn't matter.'

The QBP itself is enormously exhausting. Hundreds of people all talking at the tops of their voices, scores of harassed waiters and waitresses rushing about trying to keep glasses topped up, members of the Embassy trying desperately to remember peoples' names and make introductions. A military band sweltering in the heat.

Eventually the torture is over but everyone knows that in a few months' time the whole process of polishing and refining the QBP invitation list will start all over again. It is the social equivalent of painting the Forth Bridge.

One is very nostalgic for the days when the Embassy simply put an advertisement in the local paper, announcing the date of the QBP and saying that all British subjects in the area were welcome. The starting gun would go off at six, the guests would pile into the drink for two hours and then at eight the Service Attachés would go round saying 'Right you! You've had enough! Time you were off!'

Party Games

Embassies regard visits by MPs with almost as much ambivalence as they regard visits by Royalty. The problem is the unpredictability. Many MPs are charmers but some are decidedly tricky. Heated arguments with Ambassadors are not unknown (one colleague called these encounters the Elected versus the Selected), and some Members imagine that the inquisitorial ways of Select Committees are the norm throughout the world. A Parliamentary visit can be so stressful that the Head of Post prays for a Three Line Whip in London and when these prayers are answered, he can barely conceal his delight as he waves the dejected Parliamentarians off at the airport.

But other Parliamentary visits go like a dream. Sparring partners from opposite sides of the House, under the influence of Ambassadorial rum punch and the rhythm of a steel band, swear each other eternal friendship, while local politicians make fulsome speeches about what an honour it is to be visited by the Mother of Parliaments. Everyone positively glows.

But the inescapable fact is that the culture of British politics is confrontational: the cut and thrust of debate at Question Time, the constant vigilance for gaffes by the other side which provide opportunities to emit howls of derision, even the layout of the debating chamber—all these produce a combative state of mind. One cannot really expect MPs when they travel abroad to leave their boxing gloves in their lockers in the Palace of Westminster.

Westminster's trench warfare was transferred to a foreign field in a rather novel way during one of my postings. The occasion was a buffet dinner being given by my Ambassador for a delegation of 30 MPs. He was a generous host and the wines were flowing. Two MPs from one of the major parties were just about to tuck into their hors d'oeuvre when they spotted a signed photograph of a former Prime Minister from the Opposition close by on a side table.

"Now we can't have that looking at us while we eat, can we?" said one "It'll just have to go."

"Quite right," said the other. "It'll just have to go."

And with that the hapless Prime Minister was seized and dropped into a nearby waste paper basket. This bit of mischief was seen by a member of the opposing party who rose from his chair, grabbed a portrait of a luckless ex-Foreign Secretary from the other side and dropped it into the waste paper basket.

This game of consigning signed photographs of leading British politicians, past and present, to waste paper baskets could have gone on until the whole of the Ambassador's collection, accumulated over a long career, had been binned; but it was brought to a halt by the intervention of the Ambassador himself, who had been tipped off about what was going on (some say by a Liberal Democrat, but I am sure that is a calumny).

"Now chaps," he said "you've had your fun" (the Ambassador had once taught in a large public school). "The score, I see, is one all. I suggest you retrieve my pictures, return them to where you found them, and go back to having your dinner."

Responding to this smack of firm government, the delinquents fished the pictures out of the bins and placed them back in their rightful positions. The Ambassador rewarded them by beckoning a the waiter to refill glasses.

It was just as well that no arch republicans had been present. Feelings could have run very high indeed if photographs of the Royals had started ending up in the bin. There might even have been a bout of fisticuffs. As so often in diplomacy, one had to be grateful for small mercies.

Pooling Resources

THE BREAK UP OF THE Soviet Empire has created a sudden need for countries such as the UK to establish embassies in the numerous states which have, overnight, achieved independence. Ways of doing this as economically as possible are being looked at in London, Paris and Bonn. Savings could be achieved if we and, say, the Dutch shared the rent on a property in Tbilisi or Baku and resources might be pooled on the provision of consular services.

When I mentioned all this to my Latin American colleague, Enrico, today, he said that none of this was new to him. He already had experience of working closely with the embassy of another country. This had happened when he had been the Number 2 in Copenhagen and the embassy of another Spanish speaking country had had offices in the same building.

It had struck him as absurd that there were two embassies working away, writing political and economic reports each week for their capitals, often drawing on exactly the same sources, and only a few metres away from one another. It would be much more rational if one week one embassy did the political reporting while the other did the economic, and vice versa the following week. He stressed that it was necessary that each embassy kept its hand in on both subjects in case of telephone enquiries or ministerial visits from capitals.

Enrico invited his opposite number in the other embassy to lunch and pointed out the absurdity of the present situation. He outlined his suggestion for putting an end to it. The man was in total agreement. 'Que buena idea!' he exclaimed. His Embajada would definitely play its part.

The arrangement was an enormous success. Each embassy received a letter of congratulation from its capital for the speed with which its reports were now coming through and, with the time saved as a result of the rationalisation, the diplomatic staff in both embassies were able to take longer lunch hours and devote more time to getting to know prominent Danes. Knowing Enrico, I guessed that this was, in fact, a code for tall blondes.

The story put me in mind of Graham Greene's 'Our Man in Havana' where Wormald, a very reluctant M16 agent, sends drawings of the innards of a vacuum cleaner back to his masters in London and is showered with congratulations for achieving a great espionage coup.

The next time I run into the Australians, I'll put a proposition to them. If they agree, I'll have more time for getting to know prominent Germans.

The Rat Pack

NOTHING EVOKES MORE MIXED FEELINGS in a diplomatic post than the news that it is to be the recipient of a Royal Visit, small or large. Of course, there is great anticipation at the prospect of meeting members of the Royal Family, but there is also an acute concern that nothing will go wrong. Careers can be made or broken on the wheel of a Royal visit. Knighthoods and decorations can follow a major visit, but so can black marks on annual reports or even 'In Confidence' letters to Personnel.

Every minute of the RV has to be programmed, every movement choreographed. The quality of the mattresses, the view from the bedroom and the time it takes to run a bath, all have to be checked. Menus, placements, motorcades and guest lists become the daily fare of the Post.

There are discussions about which High Commission child should be presented first. Should it be 'the senior child' or a child from the ranks? And during the visits of some Royals the Head of Post takes precedence, as he is the Queen's Representative. One ambassador was heard to say, 'My Jaguar has to go first as I am the Queen'.

Many RVs attract Fleet Street's team of Royal watchers, those commentators, reporters and photographers who do nothing but Royal stories. Commendably without illusions about themselves, they call themselves the Rat Pack. The unspoken hope of every Rat Packer is that there will be some gaffe, snub or mishap which can be turned into massive headlines, ideally accompanied by many photographs.

I have experience of an overseas visit by a Royal couple which went very well for the Pack—that is, it went very badly for the Embassy. On the Sunday morning the car containing the Royal couple ran into the back of a police car during a high speed dash from the Ambassador's Residence to the Anglican church, with the result that the Royal car arrived at the church with dents in its front bumper and radiator. The Pack swarmed round, taking pictures and firing questions. I was reminded of a kill in the Serengeti Game Reserve. The story was no longer 'Royals attend Matins', it was now 'Royals in Foreign Limo Crash'.

The Pack was, of course, still hovering at the airport on the couple's departure. Who knows? A protocol man's trousers might fall down between the airport building and the aircraft steps. Eventually that blissful moment arrived when no-one's trousers had fallen down and the Queen's Flight aircraft had completed its wheels up and was heading for England.

As the plane disappeared from view, one of the Royal watchers turned to me and extended his hand, 'It's been a great visit. Without that car shunt outside the church, there wouldn't have been much of a story. Thanks for everything'. I thought for one moment he was going to get his chequebook out but disappointingly he didn't.

A Rest for Gavin

All UK-based staff in British Consulates are required to take their turn as duty officer, receiving calls out of office hours or at weekends from British subjects with problems or enquiries. For a few hours these calls can plunge one into the lives and crises of one's fellow countrymen abroad.

I once received a telephone call late at night from a police station in the south of our area. The policewoman said that they had just detained a young British couple as they had been trying to board a train. There were strong grounds for believing that the couple had been trying to leave town to avoid having to pay a hefty hotel bill which they had run up over several weeks. The policewoman said that the English lady wanted to speak to me. The voice that came on the line was confident and calm, its possessor seemingly quite unaffected by the shock of having been taken to a police station.

The young woman said that her name was Melanie and that I had to get her and her friend, whose name was Gavin, released, because they were innocent. I said that of course I accepted that they might be innocent, but I did not have the power to command the German police to release her and her friend.

'Why not?' she said, 'you're the British Consul'. I replied that a German Consul in England could not get a German couple released in similar circumstances from a British police station. 'That's different,' replied Melanie. I decided not to enter into a debate on this point.

I explained to her that they would have to spend the night in the police station and that in the morning a German magistrate would come to decide whether they had any charges to answer. Melanie then said that if I couldn't arrange for them to be released, I could at least arrange for her and Gavin to sleep in the same cell. The police were going to put them in separate cells and they never slept apart. I said I would do my best but I was not optimistic. It was standard practice for men and women to be put in separate cells, even in England (indeed, especially in England).

As I had predicted, my intervention with the policewoman was not successful—the couple would have to spend the night in the police station and separated. The police lady said the word 'getrennt' very firmly. I broke this news to Melanie who said she had been expecting this answer. She had clearly abandoned all faith in British Consuls.

I told her that one of my colleagues would telephone the police station in the morning to find out what the magistrate had decided. If they were detained any further, a Vice-Consul would travel down to see them. I said I was sorry I had not been able to do more for her and her friend Gavin, and rather lamely wished them good luck and good night.

As I put the 'phone down, I judged that the chances of a letter of complaint from Melanie or her MP to the Foreign Office complaining that we had failed to secure her and Gavin's release were there but probably minimal, but I definitely did not rule out a letter from the silent Gavin, saying that, thanks to the total impotence of British Consuls in the late twentieth century, he had been able to get his first good night's rest in several weeks.

Sadly, no such letter ever came.

THE SPOTTERS SPOTTED

Spot the Spook

JOURNALISTS OFTEN ALLEGE THAT HIDDEN among the staff of British posts abroad are members of SIS, Britain's overseas intelligence service. The service is also known as MI6. Common sense dictates that these allegations must be correct. Intelligence agencies operate under many guises and from many addresses, and basing their operatives in selected embassies, legations and consulates offers many obvious advantages. SIS is no exception, and some of the UK's posts around the world are among the favourite perches of SIS's hawks and owls, but of course no official spokesman will ever confirm this.

Many Ambassadors were far from happy when they learned that they were going to a post where there was an SIS covey roosting in the rafters. They feared that derring-do operations launched from the Embassy would lead to horrendous diplomatic incidents. But these fears are a thing of the past. The Service's Bulldog Drummond types have long since retired and a more cautious breed has taken their place. Shame, many would say.

The SIS men and women posted to diplomatic missions are indistinguishable from the full time diplomats. They have cover jobs in straight diplomacy and they come from similar social and educational backgrounds. Some are under such deep cover that even their colleagues in the mission know nothing of the double lives they are leading.

Identifying the SIS man in an Embassy (and there may not even be one) can be so difficult that playing "tinker, tailor, soldier, spy" round the table during the Chancery meeting is as good a method as any.

Foreign governments expend a great deal of time and energy in trying to spot who the British spooks are, but more often than not they get it wrong. I heard of a man in front of whom a foreign power dangled several attractive girls in the mistaken belief that he was the resident MI6 man. He believed it was due to the fact that he wore shoes with steel tips. On the strength of this, another man in the Chancery took up wearing steel tipped shoes but he waited in vain for the girls. None were unleashed in his direction.

And in their turn, the SIS men play spot the spook, trying to pinpoint who precisely their oppos are in other embassies and going to great lengths to get alongside suspects. A good third of those taking part in diplomatic corps tennis tournaments are intelligence officers eyeing each other up over the net, and if you get landed with the organisation of a diplomatic corps outing, you can always rely on a good turn out from the intelligence community. A long coach journey to some distant Schloss or coffer dam provides an excellent opportunity for getting to know Boris, Mehmet or Go Chin Lee.

Spy fiction has created an enormous number of misconceptions about the world of espionage. One is that spies are always bumping people off. I once asked a retired SIS man about assassination over a lunch at the Travellers. He said that the only assassination he had ever been involved in, or even heard of, had occurred when he was en poste in a North African country. The local MI6 team had had access to a flat overlooking the harbour from which they had been able to observe the comings and goings of all shipping.

But irritatingly the local municipality had decided to line the sea front with fully grown palm trees in an attempt to attract more tourism, and one of these trees was in a critical position, blocking the view from the flat of the harbour entrance. And so an MI6 operative had had to carry out an assassination of the tree, injecting it at dead of night over a period of several days with an extra powerful herbicide specially concocted by MI6's boffins in London. Eventually the wretched tree had expired and been carted away for cremation. The operation successfully completed, MI6 had been able to resume their ship spotting.

Das Britische Replacement Oar

Stick to Cricket

Invariably when one arrives in a new Post, one is approached by the local cricket club, which always has a name like the Accra Ramblers or the Maharuti Strollers, and asked if one wants to join. I once made the mistake of saying that I was a rowing man and that I planned to join the local rowing club. This brush off was not very well received by the British secretary of the Dornbusch Grasshoppers.

Not long after I had joined the rowing club, whose name was the Frankfurter Rudergesellschaft Germania, I presented myself for rowing and was allocated to a crew which was going to use an old clinker-built VIII called the *Deutschland*. As I took my oar down to the landing stage, I noticed that it too carried the name *Deutschland*. I was assigned the Number 2 seat, we launched *Deutschland* and, after adjusting our stretchers, we set off towards Griesheim which lay six kilometres downstream. I was the only non-German on board.

We had not been rowing for more than ten minutes when suddenly there was a sharp cracking sound. As I had driven off the stretcher at the beginning of the stroke, I had broken the oar or, looking at it another way, the oar had snapped while I had been using it. The rest of the crew had of course to stop rowing.

In an effort to make light of what I had done, I said in German, 'Now here you see the strength of an Englishman! He can break an oar in two!' I was in fact acutely embarrassed. This was the rowing equivalent of breaking a piece of your host's china at a dinner party. Not only had I broken an oar but, the only foreigner on board, I had broken an oar labelled *Deutschland* and, worse still, I had brought the entire *Deutschland* to a halt. What would the Foreign Office say? They might say that, in the first place, as a British Consul, I should not have been sitting in a boat with the name of a foreign country.

My piece of bravado drew ripostes from the rest of the crew. Number 3 said it had nothing to do with my strength: all the oars were old and mine had just been the first to give way. Number 5 said the oars had almost certainly been made in England. Number 6 said they would carry on to Griesheim; I could swim back to the boat house. Number 4 muttered something about 'Britische Sabotage'.

Satisfied they had saturated me with their return fire, the rest of the crew turned *Deutschland* round and slowly rowed her back to the boathouse with me sitting somewhat ignominiously as a passenger and holding the fractured oar.

Back at the boat house I picked up a replacement oar which, thankfully, had no name like *Berlin* or *Siegfried* written on it, and we were able to row *Deutschland* down to Griesheim and back without mishap, and apparently without any recrimination. I assumed that all had been forgiven.

However, when the following Saturday I reported for rowing, I found myself allocated to a boat called *Bonzo* which was even older and heavier than *Deutschland* and with an extraordinary assortment of fellow oarsmen. Perhaps this was all pure chance but, as I helped to lug *Bonzo* the twelve kilometres to Griesheim and back, I could not dispel the thought that *Bonzo* was the sort of ignominious sounding boat in which you might put sundry beginners, weight watchers and foreign saboteurs.

Now none of this would have happened if I had signed up with the Dornbusch Grasshoppers.

SOGOP

I WAS ONCE TOLD A story about a man who said his career had been ruined by SOGOP. The man had not done badly, he'd finished as a Consul-General in one of the bigger European cities but he would have liked to have finished as an Ambassador somewhere. When asked to explain what exactly was SOGOP, this was his reply.

"My first posting in the Service was as Third Secretary in Bangkok and, one afternoon not long after I arrived, I was sent by my Ambassador to sit in the UK seat at a SEATO conference. The temperature was infernally high and the discussion dragged on interminably. My attention wandered and I started doodling on my pad.

Suddenly a loud voice from the chair boomed out, 'And what does the delegate of the United Kingdom think?'

I hadn't the foggiest idea on what I had to venture an opinion and in desperation looked at my pad for inspiration. There I had scrawled 'SOGOP'.

'SOGOP', I replied.

'SOGOP?' boomed the voice from the chair. 'And what is SOGOP?'

'It's a well known British saying,' I stammered. 'It means "Shit Or Get Off the Pot". S-O-G-O-P. Stop dithering. Make up your mind'.

There was a stunned silence and all heads turned to look at the United Kingdom. After what seemed like an eternity, the chairman said icily, 'We will note the United Kingdom's views and move on'.

Needless to say, and very happily, the chairman did not ask the United Kingdom its views again and I thought that that was the end of the matter—but unfortunately it wasn't. Word about my SOGOP performance got back to the Embassy. The Counsellor said he thought it had been rather a good intervention—there was far too much talking and not enough doing in SEATO—but the Ambassador was hopping mad. He wanted to have me sent back to London with a recommendation that I was unsuited to a career in diplomacy, but the Counsellor, to my eternal gratitude, managed to calm him down and I survived.

But I'm quite convinced that SOGOP dogged my career forever afterwards and that I was always known in Personnel as 'that SOGOP chap'.

If it really is true that SOGOP had blighted the man's career it is most unfair. SOGOP is a very good principle with which to go through life, and certainly every international organisation in the world should have 'SOGOP' written at the top of every document and a sign reading 'SOGOP' in every committee room.

The Square Cyril

ONE OF THE GREAT SADNESSES of life in the Service is that every three or four years one has to part from people one has grown to like—in one's own mission or in other missions or in the local community. Paradoxically, these partings can (but not always) be hardest in the grimmest postings. Shared experiences of electricity cuts, road blocks and taps producing only brown water can create bonds which are far stronger than those in countries where the trains run on time and the rubbish is removed every other day.

The problem is then how to stay in touch with the large number of people one has got to know and like in the course of several postings. Many people use the 'round robin', a duplicated letter which might be sent to as many as 40 or 50 people. Christmas time is the favourite season for the despatch of the round robin, and they are almost invariably along the following lines.

'Jonathan got his promotion to Counsellor in June and we arrived here in September. People in the Mission couldn't have been more helpful when we arrived. Lady P came round personally to see if there was anything I needed when I was unpacking. The house is vast and the staff we've inherited are a dream. We've given several dinner parties and everything ran like clockwork. Jonathan's loving the work: he's head of the political section and we've already been at the homes of three leading politicians. Access seems incredibly easy here.

'We've also done two trips into the interior. Quite fascinating. The hill people still retain their way of life and the scenery is truly spectacular. We're planning to spend Christmas on the coast when the children come out. Both are loving boarding school. Tamsin got five As in GCSE and Robert is in the under 14s rugby side at his school. We can't wait to see them get off the plane on Saturday.'

One receives so many letters in this vein that one yearns for one that goes like this.

'We've been in this posting for only seven months but we're already counting the days until it's over. Morale here is absolutely rock bottom. The head of post feels he should have got something better and does the bare minimum. The Counsellor's wife left him earlier in the year and he's hitting the bottle. The domestic staff steal, there are constant shortages and driving around at night is so dangerous that all entertaining is done at lunch time. To get to the only beauty spot, you need an armed guard.

Peter looked in the Seniority List when he was in London in August and found that he's now the fourth oldest Second Secretary in the Office. This means our next posting will almost definitely be another hell hole. The children have at last settled at school (thank goodness, after Judy's near expulsion for smoking pot last year) but Tim failed two of his A levels and will have to go to a crammer. This place is so awful, we'll be flying to them at Christmas. We can't wait.'

If the first sort of letter is a Round Robin, then the second sort must be a Square Cyril. One suspects in fact that there's many a Square Cyril hiding beneath a Round Robin.

ONE OF THE FLEET'S CRUISERS

page 40

The Submariners

SERVING IN THE FOREIGN SERVICE is not unlike being in the Navy. About two thirds of one's career is spent at sea, serving in some of our missions abroad, and the other third at home in the Foreign Office, in the Admiralty as it were.

Being sent to a new post resembles being sent to a ship; new comrades, new accommodation, new part of the world, new chef de mission. Heads of posts, like ships' commanders, vary enormously in personality, temperament and reputation. Some have reputations as workaholics, others as fusspots, some as charmers (one Ambassador was widely known as 'DSA'—Darling Sir Antony), others as martinets.

In the 1960s, an Ambassador in a European capital had a man sent home for starting to walk up a flight of stairs as he, the Ambassador, was walking down it. Being sent home is the FO equivalent of a keel hauling. The man sent home had probably committed other crimes apart from this gross breach of stair etiquette, such as being seen several times in the town without his hat.

Some heads of post are ex-naval officers. They take easily to the way of life and they bring with them the language of the Navy. Once, when I was on a visit to a big Embassy to prepare for a Prime Ministerial visit, the Ambassador said to me, 'Are you getting the co-operation you need from the crew? Let me know if you want me to get out the lash.'

Overseas posts, like the ships of a fleet, vary greatly in their size and fire power: there are the battleships and aircraft carriers like Paris, Washington and Berlin and the heavy cruisers like Rome, Moscow and Tokyo and so on down the line to the destroyers and corvettes. The fleet's minesweepers are the consulates, as they have to defuse tricky consular cases before they attract the attention of tabloid journalists and constituency MPs.

I was once in a small post which I would describe as a destroyer, but which the Ambassador was always trying to convert into a cruiser. At regular intervals through the year he'd say, 'We must send more telegrams! We've only sent 35 this year and it's already May! Any report which could go as a letter or a telegram, make it a telegram! We must get more visibility!' which, of course, really meant more visibility for him.

Personally, I can't think of anything worse than more visibility. One wants to be in one of those posts which London forgets, like a tiny consulate in a remote part of the former Austro-Hungarian empire or a Graham Greene embassy in the tropics which people think have been long closed down, until halfway through the year they send their second telegram. Having almost nil visibility, these are the submarines of the diplomatic fleet. I'd say that a submariner is the thing to be.

FOSTERING RELATIONS WITH THE LOCALS

page 42

Third World Carlton

SEX IS A SENSITIVE SUBJECT in any walk of life but in the British Foreign Service it has high octane sensitivity. This is because sex can all too easily lead people into the FO's three top danger zones: BRS (becoming a risk to security), SFI (succumbing to financial impropriety) and BSD (bringing the Service into disrepute)

Anxiety about the first peril was naturally at its height during the Cold War, and secretaries going to embassies behind the Iron Curtain were told that it would be far better if they didn't have sex at all but if they really insisted, it should be confined to NATO members only.

At this time FO Security recruited a team of retired RAF and Army officers and tasked them to grill every member of the Service about their sex lives, at least every three years, and to flag up all those they thought might let a Red into their Bed. The lucky people they flagged up were then spared Moscow, Warsaw and Peking.

The second peril has nothing to do with the Cold War but lots to do with the poverty of FO men when they are in London. When abroad, their allowances enable them to keep up with the life style of the beguiling Consuela Isobella de Rodrigez but, once the couple are in the flat in Muswell Hill, it is a very different story, and there have, sadly, been several cases of debt and even one or two of embezzlement. The embezzlers have landed in Pentonville and the Consuelas have gone back to Tegucigalpa. The old practice of recruiting people with private incomes did have something to commend it.

The third peril is the one beset with most controversy. Exactly how do you define conduct liable to bring the Service into disrepute? One man's promiscuity can easily be another's gentle philandering, and behaviour which is disreputable in Croydon may not be in Kampala. The most celebrated exponent of this principle was Third World Carlton. He was so called because the Wingcos and Colonels had decreed that he should never serve in Europe, let alone behind the Iron Curtain. He went on to have six postings on four continents, with a local girlfriend in each and babies in three.

In one of his posts the local British community wrote to the FO complaining about the unbecoming behaviour of the High Commissioner, and demanding his recall. In response TWC forwarded a letter from the island's foreign minister which said that Mr Carlton was held in very high esteem by the local population and that among his many attributes, he was the first HE who could reggae decently, (which of course meant indecently). The Under-Secretary, fortunately a man with an enlightened set of priorities, agreed that Carlton was on the island to foster relations with the locals, and not with a bunch of British tax exiles with a colonial view of the world, and so Carlton survived.

As one would expect, the French are much more relaxed than the British about these things. It can easily happen at a French reception, after all the bigwigs have left, that your host will sidle up and whisper: 'Ne partez pas. Ça va chauffer' ('Stick around. Things are going to hot up.') and, within twenty minutes, two taxis have arrived full of girls in a party mood and a third with a three-man rumba combo.

Third World Carlton was one of the very few British Heads of Post who could seriously rival the French on the louche party stakes. His rumbas and sambas will be sorely missed throughout the Third World, and the Wingcos will secretly miss his three yearly revelations.

COMMERCIAL SECRETARY   DEFENCE ATTACHÉ   FIRST SECRETARY, CHANCERY

page 44

Writhing for the Float

THERE IS AN ACTIVITY WHICH goes on in all large UK diplomatic missions known as 'writing for the float'.

The float is a file containing copies of the letters, minutes and reports which members of the various sections of the Embassy have written during the course of the week. It is so called because it is circulated or 'floated' around the Embassy. There is a Chancery float, a Defence float, a Commercial float, a Consular float, and so on.

The Chancery float enables the Ambassador and Deputy Head of Mission to have some idea of what their staff are doing and to put comments in the margins of letters such as: 'Please speak!', 'Spelling!' or 'No!'. And because these senior officers write annual reports on the Chancery staff and to some extent base their assessments on what they see on the float, it is vital for each officer to have written a decent number of letters each week.

Usually quite enough is going on locally for there to be a natural supply of topics for the Chancery to report on, but occasionally there is a lull and an anguished cry goes up, 'Oh God! I haven't got anything on the float this week!' A flurry of activity ensues as people cast around for topics to write to London about.

Rather like foreign correspondents needing to file copy to meet a deadline, they scan the local newspapers for ideas, or they ring contacts in the Ministry of Foreign Affairs for a read-out on the host government's policy towards South America or on biological warfare. They then feverishly put pen to paper or fingers to the keyboard. This activity is called 'writing for the float'. Although he was well used to turning out essays at school and at university, one colleague found the whole business so stressful that he used to call it 'writhing for the float'.

It is also known for complete fiction to be written. Another colleague invented a story about a 'dung for oil' swap: the country in which we were stationed, the Netherlands, was drowning in surplus dung and he reported that it was about to be shipped to a North African country in exchange for oil. London didn't even query the bit about swine dung being included in the consignments.

The reports which result from these efforts are seldom, if ever, acknowledged by the Foreign Office or the other Whitehall Departments they might go to, but this does not upset the writers one bit as, of course, the purpose is not to write for London, but for the float. Indeed, there was one daredevil who sometimes did not even bother to put his float fodder letters in the diplomatic bag. On the extremely rare occasions that the Ambassador asked if he had had any reaction to one of these floated but unsent letters, he'd say, 'I'll chase them up, Ambassador. They're an idle lot in London.'

ABROAD, ONE IS SOMEBODY

The Toads

THERE WAS A TIME WHEN there were many aristocrats in the Foreign Service, dating perhaps from the days when it was thought that only aristocrats really knew how to behave, but now there are very few. I can think of only about half a dozen in today's service, if that. But being in the Foreign Service is still quite a good entrée for meeting aristocrats.

Primarily this happens abroad. At home one is nobody, a nine-to-six, commuting civil servant, turning out briefs for Ministers and answering Parliamentary Questions. But abroad one is somebody. Heaven knows why, because one is essentially the same person, but it is all about trappings. At home one has no trappings, abroad one has numerous trappings—a large house, an entertainment allowance, a card with a fancy title, a car with special registration plates. As a result one can move in circles which wouldn't give one a second glance at home. It's therefore probably as well then that, at regular intervals, we are brought back to London to have our noses rubbed in ministerial briefs.

I once attended a dinner party in Germany where I was the only person present who had no title. I didn't even have a polysyllabic name. My host was a baron with an English mother and my hostess was a Prinzessin in her own right.

I found myself seated next to another princess who was the châtelaine of an estate on the Rhine near Wiesbaden which has extensive vineyards, producing the grape for a well known brand of Sekt. She had been born in St Petersberg which her family had left at the time of the Revolution. Subsequently educated by English and French governesses, and married to a member of a leading Austrian family, she was fluent in Russian, French, German and English.

At one point I asked her whether she had been back to Russia since the collapse of the Soviet Union. She said she had and that moreover she had made regular visits during the Soviet period. I remarked that the new Russia appeared to be in the hands of ex-KGB thugs and gangster bosses.

She said this was so but that it did not worry her.

'Of course the toads are in control at the moment: toads always dominate in times of chaos but, in time, the toads will become less toad-like. Because toads have money, they marry beautiful women. They will send their children to expensive schools in England and they will start to buy expensive pictures at Christie's. It is happening already. And in two generations they will be tall, good-looking, cultured gentlemen.

'My own ancestors were assuredly toads. All aristocratic families began as toads. It is like evolution in miniature. Originally we all crawled out of the mud.'

As I sat at that silver-laden table, drinking burgundy and eating gigot d'agneau, I reflected that this charming lady had no idea that I had crawled out of the Foreign Office canteen but I was quite sure that had she known, she would not have minded one bit.

The Strasbourg Gargoyles

STRASBOURG, AS THE HOME OF the Council of Europe and the European Court of Human Rights, is a place where many grievances are aired: Kurds come here to demonstrate against Turkey, Gibraltarians to demonstrate against Spain and Chechnyans to protest about the military in Russia.

And then there are the lone vigils, some of them very sad in their futility. There was the Croat who sat in his car day and night across the road from the Palais de l'Europe with notices in the windscreen detailing some injustice he claimed his government had inflicted upon him. There is the Polish lady who comes every summer to protest outside the Court against its rejection of her complaint against Sweden. She sits all day, with her placards fixed to the fence, until sunset when she packs them into a suitcase which she wheels away to wherever she lodges.

Other grievances are aired, only in a more sophisticated manner, within the Palais building, often to the accompaniment of champagne and canapés. The Greeks have mounted an exhibition in the upper foyer of the main hall, reiterating their demand for the Elgin Marbles to be removed from the British Museum and returned to Athens. This evening I attended the opening reception.

If one cares to read the panels carefully, Elgin is portrayed as something of a scoundrel. He is alleged to have bribed Turkish Ottoman officials to allow him to remove the Marbles. It is claimed that his workmen performed very crude surgery when making the removal, leaving the Parthenon damaged and, apparently worst of all, he wanted the Marbles solely for his own personal enjoyment on his private estate.

All of this may well be true; I am not qualified to judge but, finding myself talking to one of the Greeks, I felt I had to produce one or two of our standard defences of Elgin.

'But for Elgin, the Marbles could well have been broken up to provide masonry for nearby tavernas and dwellings.' The Greek said this was nonsense. The Greeks had always deeply revered the Parthenon.

'And to give you an idea of how outrageous was Elgin's action,' he went on, 'what he did in 1801 was like your Ambassador today climbing up the scaffolding of the cathedral in Strasbourg, cutting off all the best gargoyles and taking them back to England. That would be quite unacceptable, would it not?'

I replied that put like that, Elgin's deed did seem rather high handed, but privately I thought that the UK Delegation must immediately start getting our man, who must weigh all of seventeen stone, in training for scaffolding climbing and gargoyle removal. We could well shortly need a replacement for the Marbles.

Mr Wilkinson

TWICE EVERY YEAR SINCE 1954, spring and autumn, Mr Wilkinson has visited his customers in Germany. Mr Wilkinson is a London tailor with a business in St George's Square. In advance of each visit to Germany, he sends his customers a printed card setting out his itinerary and they then stand by for his telephone call.

Over the years Mr Wilkinson has had a number of British diplomats serving in Germany among his clients and 'just out of courtesy', as he puts it, he always sends the local head of mission a copy of his card—just in case he can be of service, you understand.

I had spoken to Mr Wilkinson several times on the telephone but had never met him. As opportunities to do so were fast running out, I made an appointment to visit him last Tuesday at the Frankfurter Hof hotel where, he told me, he always stays when in Frankfurt. Mr Wilkinson met me at the lift on the fourth floor and escorted me to the small, quiet room at the back of the hotel which, he said, he always takes.

Samples of cloth and tweed were set out in neat rows on a bed. The wardrobe was filled with suits ready for final fitting or delivery. Over a cup of tea, Mr Wilkinson lamented the decline of British diplomatic sartorial standards. Anticipating Mr Wilkinson's very high standards in these matters, I had put on my best Austin Reed off the peg clothes, so I hoped that he did not find me too wanting.

He told me that he had learned German whilst a member of the occupying forces in Austria at the end of the war, and so he had decided to extend the family bespoke tailoring business into Germany. A more courteous and gentler occupier than Mr Wilkinson would be hard to imagine. He said he never advertised. New business came solely by recommendation. He had benefited from the high esteem in which good English tailoring was held by many of Germany's leading families, lawyers and bankers.

At one point Mr Wilkinson lowered his voice, as if fearing we might be overheard. 'You know the years take their toll, Mr Hall. They take their toll. I watch sadly as the girth becomes greater, the shoulders narrower, the stature smaller and the stoop more prominent. It's inescapable, Mr Hall. It's inescapable.'

I almost suggested that it was partly the changing shapes of his customers which helped to keep him in business, but stopped myself when I realised that his regret at the ravages wrought by time on his clients was totally sincere.

After tea, I took my leave of Mr Wilkinson. There was absolutely no rancour that I had not ordered a suit. I was extremely pleased I had made the effort to meet Mr Wilkinson. Twenty years hence, there will be no Mr Wilkinsons.

Biographical note

Michael Hall

Michael Hall was born in Cape Town in 1942. He was educated at schools in Swaziland, South Africa, Kenya and Canterbury and at Cambridge University where he read languages. His late father was a member of the Colonial Service in Africa, and his mother was born in what was at the time Southern Rhodesia.

He entered the Central Office of Information in 1969 and then the Foreign Office in 1973. In 1984 he transferred to the Diplomatic Service. He served in Rhodesia, the Netherlands, Germany and with the UK Delegation to the Council of Europe in Strasbourg.

He greatly enjoyed the variety of his various stints in the FCO in London: arranging conferences and Ministerial visits, including the overseas travel of the Foreign Secretary and Prime Minister in the 1970s, relations with countries in Central America and in the mid-90s policy towards the British Dependent Territories in the Caribbean.

He retired from the Diplomatic Service in 2002 and has continued to live in Strasbourg. As befits someone with a peripatetic background, he divides his time between Strasbourg, Hampstead and Henley.

Pat Knights

Educated in England and Malaya, Pat joined HM Diplomatic Service (in reluctant preference to attending art college), doing time in Vienna, Cairo, Stockholm and New York. Further travels included a year in Lanzarote and several in Dubai. Whilst working in the latter as a journalist, she was persuaded to do further time – simultaneously – at the British Embassy before eventually returning to England with her husband, Peter.

Since then, apart from voluntary work – some of which involved other people doing time – Pat has now come full circle by drawing diplomatic missions and cartoons for the Foreign and Commonwealth Office Association. She lives in hope that a really interesting opportunity may yet come her way.